21 Reasons To Pray

A 21 day prayer devotional

for everyday life!

Sylvia Jackson

Copyright © 2018 Sylvia Jackson

All rights reserved. No portion of this book may be used or reproduced in any manner whatsoever without written permission of the author.

All scripture is from the King James Version of the bible.

ISBN-13: 978-1722960858

ISBN-10: 172296085X

For book inquiries please contact

Sylv89@yahoo.com

DEDICATION

Dedicated to my mother Olevia Ross, who is now with the Lord, I am grateful for her prayers. If it wasn't for her prayers I wouldn't be saved today.

To my family and friends, thank you for your love and support. To my spiritual leaders, thank you for your examples of godliness and guidance. To Jehovah God, thank you for your love, protection, and salvation.

REASON #1
Traveling Grace

I always pray before I go on a road trip. I take several trips to my hometown and it's a long drive, so I trust Father to get me there safely. I know I have Angels around me, but I still ask for His protection. After praying, I started down the road to my hometown of 'New Orleans, Louisiana. On the interstate nearest my home, I saw a man standing on the overpass with a rifle on his back, arms folded and looking at the cars traveling under the overpass. I usually keep my eyes on the road, but this caught my eyes and attention. I thought to myself, I am so glad I prayed before I left home. I began to think, why was this man standing there? Was he a sniper? Was he looking for a particular person or a random person in a car to shoot? Did he just wanted to stand on the overpass and look intimidating, to see what would happen? To this day, I don't know why he was standing there, but I'm glad I prayed. There are so many things that can happen when you travel, a car accident, someone robbing you, a random act of violence, sickness, etc. If we pray; God will protect us.

※

Father, I thank you for your protection. I know your word says, "The fear of man brings a snare, but whoever trusts in the Lord shall be safe" Proverbs 29:25. I ask that you will protect and keep me safe from the snares of man as I travel. I ask that you keep me from the rapist, the robber and the murderer. I ask that you keep me from any accident or incidents, car problems and dangers.

REASON #2
A New Day

Every day is a new opportunity to say thank you, to the Lord for all the blessings he has given to us. We should be glad and rejoice in each day. Every day that we get out of bed is a blessing. Sometimes things we went through the day before was hard. To wake up to another opportunity to have peace or see things change is wonderful. Life is a gift and we should realize that if we wake up; things can be better than it was the day before. With the dawn of a new day comes joy. We may not be joyous about everything that's happening, but we can be joyful that we have another opportunity to say thank you for life. Think of a new day as your personal invitation from God to get up and live life to its fullest.

Father, I'm grateful for this day. Thank you that "this is the day which the Lord hath made; we (I) will rejoice and be glad in it" Psalm 118:24. Thank you for waking me up to another day, so I can let you know, I appreciate all that you have done for me. I receive the joy and peace this day brings. In Jesus' name, amen.

REASON #3
Your Children

I don't have any children, but I am a teacher that knows what children go through in school. I have had to stop fights, encourage little girls of the necessity of protecting their space and bodies from little boys who would disrespect them on a daily basis. I have had to motive children that they can learn and succeed in school. Many times, I had to stress to little boys about the fact that they have to be respectful to those who have control over them. I have even told them life will not be easy for them; but they can change their mind set and be successful. With all the bullying, physical fights and school shootings; you must pray for your children daily. Please pray for ALL children, you never know when it will affect your children or children of family or friends.

Heavenly Father, I pray for my son/daughter when they are away from me. I pray for my daughter that she will not let anyone touch her inappropriately and violate her space. I pray that she will not get distracted from her education. I pray that she will get A's and B's in school. I pray for my son, that he will respect his teachers, little girls and himself in school and that he will be successful and get A's and B's in school. Father, please keep him/her from getting in trouble in and out of school. Keep him from gangs, temptations, stealing, killing, anything that will get him arrested and put in jail, or murdered. I pray for school shootings all over the world. Please protect the children from dying before their time. Thank you Lord, that my children are successful and good citizens in this world and the kingdom. In Jesus' name, amen.

REASON #4
Husband or Wife

I have been married but I am now divorced. I was married for 23 years. I saw God come in and move in the midst of my marriage. I also saw when the enemy came in and ruined my marriage. God wants man to leave his mother and father and cling to his wife. Husband and wives sometimes treat each other with disrespect, and become selfish and jealous of one another. Marriage is God's idea not man's; this is the reason satan hates marriage. Marriages have many temptations. The temptation to commit adultery, abuse each other mentally and physically, and to disregard each other needs and desires. Parents put children before their spouses. Husband and wives have to figure out how to keep God first, their marriage covenant second, and children third. I am not saying to neglect the children, because one day the children will leave and it will be just the two of you. Learn to communicate, grow, and honor each other. Marriages need to be prayed for every day. The word says in Hebrews 13:4, "Marriage is honorable and the bed undefiled."

Father, bless my marriage. Please keep my husband/wife from committing adultery, neglecting me and being selfish. Lord, let my spouse and I treat each other with respect and honor. Do not let us abuse each other in anyway. Please let us cling to each other and resist any temptations that will cause us to separate and divorce, In the name of Jesus, amen!

REASON #5
Finances

Money is not the root of all evil....it's the love of money. We have to have finances to live. We have to pay bills, feed children, buy clothes, pay rent/mortgages, pay car notes, etc. This is just the beginning of financial obligations. I don't have all of the above, but I have several financial obligations. This world requires money. As a Christian, we present tithe and offering unto the Lord so that the needs of his house and ours are met. Malachi 3:8 says, "Will a man rob God? Yet ye have robbed me. But ye say, Wherein have we robbed thee? In tithes and offerings." In order to be a blessing, you have to have finances. If a man does not work, he doesn't eat. 2 Thessalonian 3:10 says, "For even when we were with you, this we commanded you, that if any would not work, neither should he eat."

I love buying lunch for friends, blessing family, and giving to those less fortunate. One day, I want to pay electricity bills, water bills, etc. for other people. However, if I don't have money to give, I cannot be a financial blessing. Money is essential for everyday living.

Father, thank you for the monies I need to take care of my family, pay my bills and give. I don't love money, but I need it to be a blessing. Thank you that you said, "it better to give, than to receive," I want to have more than enough, so I can give and be a blessing to many in this world. In Jesus name, amen.

REASON #6
Healing and Health

We are in this flesh, therefore, healing and health is necessary. There are generational curses of diseases, such as high and low blood pressure, heart problems, diabetes, cancer, lung, liver diseases, etc. If we are sick, we can't enjoy life to its fullest. Many people live with pain yet they are able to function, but that is not God's best. Isaiah 53:5 says, "But he was wounded for our transgressions, he was bruised for our iniquities: the chastisement of our peace was upon him; and with his stripes we are healed." Sickness and diseases is of the devil and health and healing is of God. 3 John 1:2 says, "Beloved, I wish above all things that thou mayest prosper and be in health, even as thy soul prospereth." Father wants us to have life abundantly. John 10:10, say, "The thief cometh not, but for to steal, and to kill, and to destroy: I am come that they might have life, and that they might have it more abundantly." The enemy of our souls desires us to be sick, broken, and eventually dead. But God wants us to live in health, healing, and wholeness.

Father, thank you for providing healing and strength for my mind and body. Thank you that my body is functioning the way you intended from the foundation of the world. Thank you Jesus, that with your strips, I am healed. I decree and declare that I am healthy, whole, and that sickness and disease are not a part of my life nor will it hinder my abundant life, as my soul prospers. In Jesus' name, amen.

REASON #7
Job and Business

Everyone has challenges in their jobs or businesses. As previously stated, we have to work, pay bills, taxes, and just live. If you have a job that you enjoy, you are blessed. Even if you like your job, sometimes the people around you can be difficult to work with. If you have your own business, you have to work for customers who can be picky. I have been a teacher for several years, and sometimes it is very hard. Long hours, competitive co-workers, and paperwork can sometimes be overwhelming. Many days I had to pray about circumstances and situations, standing on the scripture that says, no weapon that formed against me shall prosper. There were many weapons that were formed, but they did not proper because God always turned it around for my good. Whether you have a job or a business, you have to pray about the people you work with, the work itself, and the money you need to live.

Father, I thank you for the blessing of my job or my business. I pray for everyone I work with. I pray that there will be peace on my job. I thank you that no weapon formed against me shall prosper. Please help me be a great employee or business owner and give me favor with my employer or customers. May my employer be pleased with my performance and let my clients or customers be satisfied with my products and services. Let my light so shine that men will see my good works and you will be glorified. In Jesus' name, amen.

REASON #8
Pastors

Pastors are very important to our spiritual growth. Jeremiah 23:1 says, "And I will give you pastors according to mine heart, which shall feed you with knowledge and understanding." Every month there are Pastors leaving the ministry; because of burnout, moral failure, and church problems. Pastors are not super humans. They are flesh and blood servants with limitations. Pastors have a lot to deal with concerning church members! Can you imagine dealing with people with different personalities, wants, and desires? They are expected to attend life and death celebrations of their members. Let's not forget they have a family of their own.

Many get caught up in immorality and have affairs with members of their churches. There are splits and divisions in churches. Additionally, church attendance and giving are down. These are only a few things pastors have to deal with and go through. They truly need our prayers.

Father, I pray for my pastor. Please give him/her strength, wisdom, knowledge and understanding to do the ministry. Give them the health and energy to serve the people you have given them. Do not let him/her fall into immorality. Give my pastor the desire to be honest and have integrity at all times. Bless his/her family and let love and compassion exude from them toward each other, their families, and their members. In Jesus' name, amen.

REASON #9
The Church

    The building is not the church, we are. So therefore, when you pray for the church, you are praying for people. There are many members in the body of Christ. Some of the leaders are apostles, prophets, evangelists, pastors, and teachers. Everyone has a function in the body of Christ. The door keepers or greeters, hospitality, and security guards are all important. So when you pray for the church, remember you are praying for people and their individual functions.

    Unity among members of the church is very important. As sisters and brothers in Christ we need to be on one accord in the body of Christ, even as we function in our individual ministries. We need to speak the word of God in order to be unified in Christ. By being unified there will be less strife and confusion in the Church.

Father, I pray for all the members of the church. Father, let the apostles establish order in the Church as well as plant churches. Allow the prophet to prophesy the truth that they hear from you. Give the pastor messages that will change the lives of your people and bring unity in the Church. Father, thank you for giving the teacher the ability to make the word of God clear. Let the greeters be friendly and anoint the music ministry to help us enter into worship and prepare the way for the sermon. In Jesus' name, amen.

REASON #10
Your Calling

When I first received Jesus in my life, I didn't know he had a calling and destiny for my life. I did not think I had any gifts or talents. My two sisters had many gifts. One sister is able to sew, and my other sister found her gift of decoration after she turned 50. Because I couldn't sew or decorate I didn't think I had talent, I found myself with no self-esteem or confidence. I always knew I wanted to teach, but didn't think that it was a talent. However, God spoke to me through a child about teaching. After that, I knew my calling.

I have a gift of explaining and making information easy to receive and learn. After I realized my calling I started teaching Bible study, VBS, and Sunday school. After many years I had a desire to teach in public school. God blessed and I became an elementary school teacher.

I encourage you to ask Father God to show you your calling. I do believe God has a time for us to walk in our calling. Once God reveals your calling you can take steps to prepare yourself until your calling manifests.

Father, I desire to serve you and your people. I want to be used by you. The word says in John 15:16 that Jesus you said in the word, "have chosen me, and ordained me, that I should go and bring forth fruit, and my fruit should remain…" Father, I ask in Jesus' name that you would reveal to me my calling, so I can prepare to do it and give you glory and honor. Thank you. In Jesus' name, amen.

REASON # 11
Deliverance From Addiction

Addictions are very serious. You can be addicted to many things, alcohol, drugs, cigarettes, medication, food, coffee, shopping, sex, and pornography. These are only a few addictions. If you are not addicted to any of these, you might have another type of addiction. In my family, my father had an addiction that I didn't want to inherit. When I was a child, my daddy was a functioning alcoholic. He would go to work Monday through Friday and would not have any problems, but on Friday night through Sunday, he would drink and become violent. As a young adult before I become saved I would socially drink on occasion on the weekends at nightclubs. I even chose not to drink coffee because I was told it was addictive. About 4 years ago I started drinking coffee, but I am not addicted. If you have an addiction, pray. God is willing and able to deliver you.

Father, I know you are able to deliver me from this addiction. I've tried to give it up, but it has me in bondage. I know this addiction is affecting me and my loved ones. Thank you for setting me free, so I can live a life of victory and peace. In Jesus' name, amen.

REASON #12
Sound Mind

I have been through a lot in my life. The world says that if you have so many life changes at one time it can cause stress. I have moved to a new home, ended a relationship, and started a new job all in one year. If I didn't have the Lord in my life, I do not know where I would be. The word says, "For God hath not given us the spirit of fear; but of power, and of love, and of a sound mind" (2 Tim.1:7). If we pray and trust God, we do not have to fear anything. Life, people, and things will challenge us. We all go through things in life. People will try to make us feel like we don't matter, that we are not worthy or important. If you let things or circumstances stress you out it can make you sick or even kill you. It is common for stress to cause heart attacks, strokes and mental issues, like depression. Through prayer, God will keep your mind sound and give you the strength to overcome any obstacles. God loves us and want us to be of a sound mind and free of stress.

Father, I thank you for a sound mind. I ask that you will deliver me from fear and stress. I thank you that I can depend on you for strength to go through anything with your help. No matter what I go through, I know that I matter, and because of you, I'm worthy and important. Thank you for your love. In Jesus' name, Amen!

REASON #13
Obedience

God wants us to trust and obey him. God wants the best for us but in order to receive His best for our lives we must obey his commandments. Job 36:11 says, "If they obey and serve him, they shall spend their days in prosperity, and their years in pleasures."

I took a break from teaching and while it was hard to return to the classroom I knew that is where God was asking me to go. It wasn't easy to trust the direction that he was leading me in, but I knew that my obedience would lead to the blessings I needed. Because I obeyed God, he opened many doors and opportunities.

Father, I forgive (their name) for hurting/betraying me. As I forgive him/her, I receive my forgiveness from you. I decree and declare today, because I am willing to obey, I am free to receive healing, blessings, favor and supernatural increases. Thank you Father for your instructions and my willingness to obey your commandments. In Jesus' name, amen!

REASON #14
Blended Family

Today blended families are very common. I personally have been a part of a blended family, so I know being in a blended family is not easy. Two families coming together to form one family requires work. One or both parents can be a step parent. If children are young it may not be hard for them to adjust, however if there are teenagers involved it may be difficult because teenagers may not be ready to let go of the fact that one of their biological parent will not be in the new home. In a traditional family, both are disciplinarians, but in a blended family the step parent may have limited authority and simply support the biological parent until the children get use to them being around. I heard that it takes about 7 years for a blended family to become fully blended. That is a long time, but not impossible to happen. I encourage you to hang in there.

Father, I pray for my blended family. I pray that everyone will respect and honor one another. I pray that my husband/wife gets along with my children and I get along with their children. I pray that we will hang in there and not give up until we are blended and one family. I pray, as adults will be patient and kind with one another and the children. Thank you for letting us be an example of a successful blended family. In Jesus' name, amen.

REASON #15
The Mind of Christ

As I was growing up I thought I was a mistake. I was born several years after my older sister. I didn't believe I was here on purpose. This thought was negative. It didn't dawn on me that God wanted me to be here. Only after I accepted Jesus into my life, I received the revelation that I am meant to be on this earth. Other stinking thinking are I'm not worthy of love, I'm not pretty enough, I'm not talented enough, I'm not educated enough, I'm not rich enough, and many other lies that the enemy tells you. Stinking thinking keeps you in bondage, and it keeps you from living life to its fullest.

To get rid of stinking thinking and to have the mind of Christ the bible gives us direction on what we should think on in Philippians 4:8, "Finally, brethren, whatsoever things are true, whatsoever things are honest, whatsoever things are just, whatsoever things are pure, whatsoever things are lovely, whatsoever things are of good report; if there be any virtue, and if there be any praise, think on these things." If we follow this scripture, we will have the mind of Christ.

Father, thank you for accepting me as I am. I realize that I am not perfect, but you love me and want me to live an overcoming life. I accept your love. I pray for the mind of Christ and the wisdom to know what I am meant to be here. I am good enough, I am an overcomer, and I will think on good things. I pray that you would help me to keep my mind on you and stop the stinking thinking. In Jesus' name, amen.

REASON #16
Prosperity

God wants us to have prosperity in our life. God wants us to have things but he does not want things to have us. Wealth is given to us for a reason. Remember it is God that gives us the power to get wealth so we can establish his covenant in this time. For He knows the thoughts that He thinks toward you, thoughts of peace, and not of evil, to give you an expected end (Jeremiah 29:11). God wants us to be in peace and not worry about life and living. They say that many People are one check from being homeless. I was there, but God didn't let it happen. The word says in 3 John 1:2, "Beloved, I wish above all things that thou mayest prosper and be in health, even as thy soul prospereth." Our Father wants us to be whole, healthy, wise and financial stable. We can pray to be prosperous in every area.

Father, thank you for prosperity. Give me the power to get wealth so that your covenant will be established. I know you want me to have things but you don't want things to have or control me. Let me have health and wealth and be financial stable, so I can be a blessing to many. Father, you get the glory, the honor, and the praise. In Jesus' Name, amen.

REASON #17
Peace

As we know, peace is priceless. Being worried, stressed, or aggravated can deprive you of peace. We should always pursue peace. Sometimes to have peace we have to back down, give in, and let go. When you have financial, family, or health problems this too can destroy your peace. When people harass and make you feel like you don't matter, know that God's peace is yours. The bible says I Ephesians 3:20 that "God is able to do exceeding; abundantly above all you can ask or think..." So let him take care of your problems and those people who would rob you of your peace.

Father, thank you for your peace, for I know that worry and stress is not of you. Sometimes, I cannot control things in my life or people, but I can pursue you and your peace at all times. I give you all my concerns about my life and I receive your tranquility and calmness. I pray for those who despitefully use and abuse me. I will cast all my care on you because I know you care for me. In Jesus' name, amen.

REASON #18
Forgiveness

Forgiveness is very important to living a life of peace. God made people in his image and likeness, but not all people are a part of his family. People are capable of doing terrible things to each other. At some time in our lives, we have been hurt, abused, and mistreated. But the problem is we cannot hold a grudge or get bitter. If we hold grudges and continue to live in bitterness; we give the abuser control of our lives. Mark 11:25 says, "And whenever you stand praying, forgive, if you have anything against anyone, so that your Father also who is in heaven may forgive you your trespasses." It's important to pray for those who do us wrong. I've been verbally and physically abused and had to forgive. It wasn't easy, but with prayer and a desire to forgive, it is possible. Give your hurt and pain to the Lord, and he will make you whole.

Father, I forgive those who have hurt me, abused me, and despitefully used me. I release them to you and ask that you help me to let go of any bitterness or anger I have toward them. Help me to understand that some of your creation does not respect or honor those you love. Father, I refuse to let others control me and my emotions. I forgive and release all those who have done me wrong. In Jesus' name, Amen.

REASON #19
Friends

True friends are rare. I have a few I can call on them when I am in trouble, when I need an opinion, resources, wisdom, knowledge, or just to talk. The word says, "A man that hath friends must shew himself friendly: and there is a friend that sticketh closer than a brother" (Prov. 18:24). I have shown myself friendly on several occasions. I have friends who didn't want any friends, but after I showed myself friendly, we have become good friends. I believe I am a good friend to my friends, but they can tell you better than I can.

It doesn't take a lot to make friends. One of my closest friends became my friend because I simply said hello and introduced myself. If you don't have any friends, take a look at yourself and become friendlier. The second part of Proverbs 18:24 say there is one who sticks closer than a brother. Jesus calls us friends. He is the ultimate friend and he will never leave you nor forsake you.

Father, thank you for calling me friend and staying closer to me than a brother. I also desire to have an earthly friend. Someone I can talk and interact with. Help me to be friendly, so I can have a friend who I can depend on and they can depend on me. In Jesus' name, amen.

REASON #20
Directions and Instructions

In life we have to make many decisions. If we depend on our imperfect selves, we will always get in trouble. Experience does bring about wisdom, but if we depend on God for directions and instructions, we can have less heartaches. Without God, our knowledge and understanding about life and living is unproductive. The word says, "Trust in the Lord with all thine heart; and lean not unto thine own understanding. In all thy ways acknowledge him, and he shall direct thy paths" (Proverbs 3:5-6). Before making any decisions in life always lean on Father for directions and instructions. He can do this in several ways in directions and instructions. He can speak directly to your spirit, give you a prophetic word, and use a friend or even a stranger. Father has spoken to me through those ways many of times. He has even spoken to me through children.

Father, I am not leaning to my own understanding. I need your help to make this life decision. Please give me your directions and instructions so that I may make the right decision. In all my ways, I acknowledge you and ask that you direct my path. Please give me your wisdom. In Jesus' name, amen.

REASON #21
The Ultimate Prayer

The most important prayer is the prayer of salvation. I know most people who will read this book is saved. However, if it was purchased for you, you may or may not be saved. If you have not accepted Jesus as your Lord and Savior, it's not too late. Jesus lived, died, and rose again so you can be free from sin. Death without salvation is eternal separation from God. The word says, "Wherefore, as by one man sin entered into the world. And death by sin; and so death passed upon all men, for that all have sinned" (Romans 5:12). The word also says, "That if thou shalt confess with thy mouth the Lord Jesus, and shalt believe in thine heart that God raised him from the dead, thou shalt be saved. For with the heart man believeth unto righteousness; and with the mouth confession is made unto salvation" (Romans 10:9-10). Father wants us all to be saved. Salvation is the most important thing you will ever receive in life.

Father, I know that I was born a sinner and in need of a savior. Father I repent of my sins. I ask that you cleanse me from all unrighteousness and come into my heart and life and be the Lord of my life. I believe in my heart that God raised Jesus from the dead and he rose on the third day. Thank you for forgiving me of my sins. In Jesus' name, amen.

If you sincerely prayed that prayer, welcome to the kingdom of God and eternal life. You will never be the same again.

MY MOST RECENT TESTIMONY AND BLESSING FOR YOU

In the process of writing this devotional I had an accident on the way to my job. I know I had prayed before the accident, because my prayer is always Father protect me from dangers unseen and seen. Keep me from the murder, robber, rapist, and the thief. Protect me from accident, from people hitting me or me hitting them.

The morning of April 17, 2018, I was driving northbound on an interstate in a nearby city when I was hit from behind. My car went into a tailspin and as I tried to hit the brakes to stop the car, it turned into the oncoming traffic. So, I was going southbound in the northbound traffic. As I called on the name of Jesus, I saw everything including two headlights in front of me. My car hit the guardrail and flipped on its side and I heard the engine go off. When I realized I was alive, I began praying to JEHOVAH God.

Someone broke the glass and asked me if I could unlock the door. When I released myself from the seatbelt, I realized I had to look up and unlock the door. I unlocked the door and I was pulled out of the car. My shoes were loose on my feet and came off. The next thing I heard was a women voice saying we can't let her walk there because there was glass on the ground. She said, "let's pick her up and carry her to the other side of the glass." They picked me up and carried me to the other side of the glass and I walked to her car.

To this day, I couldn't describe the man, because he left the scene. I think of him as my angel and the lady as my earthly angel.

I asked her why she stopped, she told me, "I would want someone to do the same for me." I prayed a lifetime blessing for her life.

May Jehovah God, Yeshua (Jesus) and the Holy Spirit answer all your prayers and may the rest of your life be blessed and prosperous!!!

Many Blessings,

Sylvia Jackson (loved and protected)

Additional Prayers

Additional Prayers

Additional Prayers

Additional Prayers

Additional Prayers

Additional Prayers

Additional Prayers